Apples

by Mary Louise Bourget
illustrated by
Nadine Bernard Westcott

 Harcourt

Orlando   Boston   Dallas   Chicago   San Diego

Visit *The Learning Site!*

www.harcourtschool.com

Ann sat with her cat.

"Will you help me?"
said Sam.

"I will help you,"
said Ann.

"We can fill the
bags," said Sam.

Ann got the bags.

"Will you help me?"
said Sam.

"I will help you,"
said Ann.